Who Makes the

Gail Skroback Hennessey, M.S.T.

Consultants

Shelley Scudder
Gifted Education Teacher
Broward County Schools

Caryn Williams, M.S.Ed.
Madison County Schools
Huntsville, AL

Publishing Credits

Dona Herweck Rice, *Editor-in-Chief*
Lee Aucoin, *Creative Director*
Torrey Maloof, *Editor*
Diana Kenney, M.A.Ed., NBCT, *Associate Education Editor*
Marissa Rodriguez, *Designer*
Stephanie Reid, *Photo Editor*
Rachelle Cracchiolo, M.S.Ed., Publisher

Image Credits: Cover & p. 1 Corbis; pp. 8, 9, 13, 17, 20 Alamy; pp. 4, 16, 19 Getty Images; p. 6 Diana Kenney; p. 5 Lynette Tanner; p. 21 (bottom) Jaden Acosta; pp. 11, 24 Stephanie Reid; p. 14 The Library of Congress [LC-DIG-ppprs-00374]; p. 12 The Library of Congress [LC-USW3-001890-D]; p. 15 North Wind Picture Archives; p. 18 The White House; All other images from Shutterstock.

Teacher Created Materials
5301 Oceanus Drive
Huntington Beach, CA 92649-1030
http://www.tcmpub.com

ISBN 978-1-4333-6972-8

Printed by: 590835
Printed in: China

Table of Contents

What Are Rules?

Do not run in the hallway. Raise your hand in class to answer a question. These may be **rules** you have heard. Rules tell what you may and may not do. Rules protect people and help them work together.

These students are breaking a rule. They are running in school.

This is a list of classroom rules.

Rules at Home

Your parents make the rules at home. If you do not follow the rules, there are **consequences** (KON-si-kwens-iz), or results. This is how you learn to make good choices.

This is a family's list of rules.

Time-Out

A time-out is a consequence. Kids take a short break. They think about how to make better choices.

This boy is in time-out.

Rules at School

Teachers make classroom rules. Walk in a straight line. Raise your hand to speak.

Principals make school rules. Be **respectful** (ri-SPEKT-fuhl). Be **responsible** (ri-SPON-suh-buhl). Be ready to learn. Be safe with your actions.

These students are standing in a straight line.

These students are holding their teacher's rules.

There are many adults at school who **enforce** the rules. They make sure the rules are followed. When you do not follow the rules, there are consequences. Your teacher may write a letter to your parents. You may miss recess.

Level 1	Level 2	Level 3
Great day!	OK day	Not a good day!

Some charts have colors. The colors help you see if you are following the rules.

Move Your Pin!

Some teachers use special charts in their classrooms. When students break a rule, they have to move their name down. They can move up for following the rules.

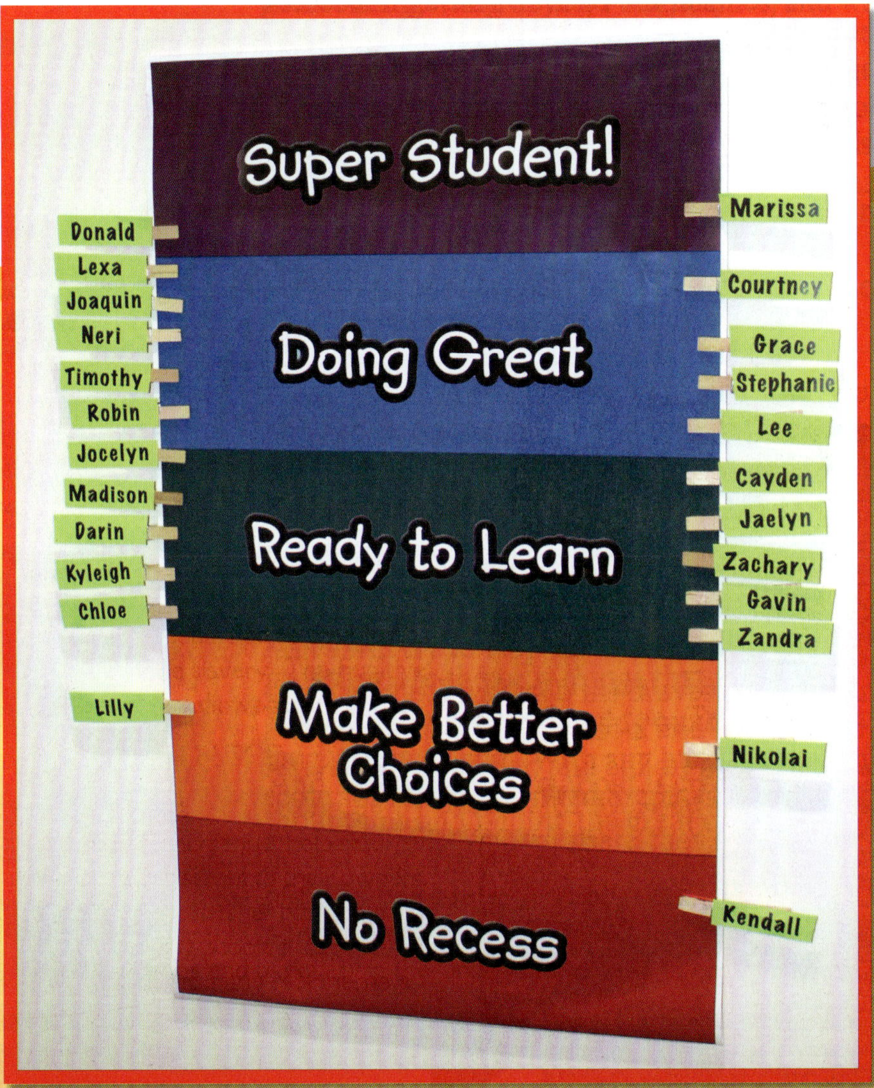

Community Rules

Communities (kuh-MYOO-ni-teez) have rules, too. Communities are places where people live and work. Communities that are big have city councils (KOUN-suhlz) that make rules. The city council is chosen by people in the community.

This is a city council from 1942.

To Protect and Serve

Police officers enforce the rules in a community. They make sure people make good choices and are safe.

This policeman is teaching bike safety.

Some communities are small. They have town meetings. At town meetings, people talk about things they need. They talk about rules and how to enforce them.

This is a town meeting long ago.

This is a town meeting today.

Country Rules

The Constitution (kon-sti-TOO-shuhn) is a list of rules for our country. It is more than 200 years old! Rules can be added or changed. They are called *amendments* (uh-MEND-muhnts).

A girl looks at the Constitution in Washington, DC.

Changes

The Constitution has been changed 27 times. There are 27 amendments.

We the People

Article. 1

United States Constitution

Our country has rules. They are called **laws**. **Congress** writes the laws. The president approves the laws. Judges decide who has broken the laws. Everyone works together. Rules and laws keep our country fair and safe.

This is Congress.

This is a judge.

Guess It!

Think about a rule at your school. Does the rule protect people? Does it help them work together? Work with a small group to act out a rule. Present your rule to your class. See if your class can guess the rule.

These kids are writing a school rule.

These kids eat in the lunchroom.
They do not eat in class.

No food in class.

Glossary

communities—places where groups of people live and work together

Congress—a group of people who make the laws for the United States

consequences—results

enforce—to make sure people follow the rules

laws—a set of rules made by a government

respectful—showing that you feel someone or something is important

responsible—able to be trusted to do what is right

rules—things that tell what you may or may not do

Index

Your Turn!

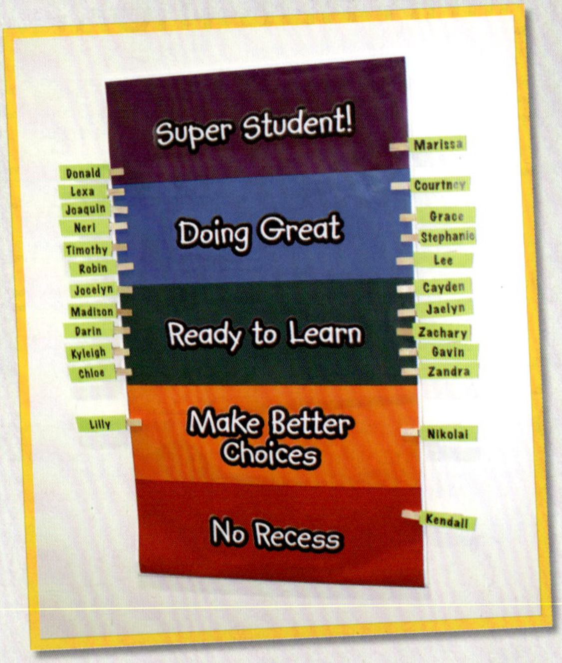

Good Job!

When kids in this class follow the rules, they get to move their names up. Talk with a friend about what happens when you follow the rules. Do you get a reward? Is your teacher happy?